From the Kitchen
Heritage Park

WOOD STOVE CUISINE

By Barb Saunders
Foodways Lead Hand (retired)

Edited by Ellen Gasser
Public Programming Coordinator

Calgary, Alberta, Canada
www.heritagepark.ca

For more information contact:
Heritage Park Society
1900 Heritage Drive SW
Calgary, Alberta, Canada
T2V 2X3

ISBN 978-0-9937094-1-8

Photography by
Claudia Lorenz Photography
Leah Brandt Photography
Ellen Gasser

Cover by Page Dynamics
Book Design by Julie Frayn

DO YOU LOVE TO COOK?

On special themed days, Heritage Park Historical Village in Calgary, Alberta hands out collectible recipe cards with tasty offerings from the past. Find more information about this, and all of Heritage Park's programs and events at www.heritagepark.ca.

The Wood Stove Cuisine cookbook is also available in e-book format.

Watch for the next cookbook in the series *From the Kitchens of Heritage Park*, as we explore and share other aspects and eras of our Foodways Programme.

TABLE OF CONTENTS

INTRODUCTION

Welcome to Heritage Park's Foodways Programme Cookbook. After receiving many requests from our guests for the recipes used at the Park in the various cooking exhibits, we decided to produce a cookbook and share a broad selection of these recipes.

The Foodways Programme, as the name implies, is all about food – how food was obtained, stored, preserved, prepared, served and consumed. In this programme, we are primarily interested in the overall approach of a society with respect to food, with a focus on the pioneers and settlers of the western interior of Canada.

Wood Stove cooking in Livingston House

In the three exhibits at Heritage Park where the Foodways Programme is primarily offered (Livingston House, Burnside Ranch House and the Rectory), each of the homes is used to represent the many other homes of the same type, time period or general location. Food patterns changed rapidly between the 1880s and 1914, and differences existed between rural and urban homes. So the programme presented in the Livingston House differs radically from the one in the Ranch House, and the programme in the Rectory is different yet again.

In the Livingston House, shortages faced by housewives (scarcity of sugar or eggs, for example) during the pre-railway period in Western Canada before 1883 are depicted. Hence, we make Rice Pudding without Eggs and substitute molasses for sugar in many of the recipes. Since dried foods such as peas were important, we will often feature Pea Soup, which

Baking in the Ranch House

also calls for salt pork, another staple of the period.

At the Burnside Ranch House, the focus is on hearty homegrown fare such as Chicken and Dumplings or Beefsteak Pie, and plenty of it would have been needed to feed the hungry ranch or farm hands. Many courses are simple but filling; desserts such as pies and puddings provide variety. Eggs, butter and cream were plentiful on the farm in 1910, but some foods were not (like orchard fruits), so substitutions are featured in recipes such as Mock Apple Pie.

In the Rectory, we focus on two food categories – invalid and convalescent fare (Barley Gruel) and tea dainties, which might have been served at a church social or women's group meeting (Egg Sandwiches, Chocolate Cookies).

Cooking in the Rectory

Traditionally, recipes were passed verbally because they required adaptations to suit local supplies and conditions.

During the time represented by Heritage Park, handwritten cookbooks were common. Often friends would write out their recipes in one another's cookbooks. By 1905, the Department of Agriculture was issuing bulletins instructing housewives in matters of "household economy." Around this time as well, food manufacturers began distributing cookbooks, which advocated the use of their products in the various recipes (*Five Roses Cookbook 1913, Robin Hood Cookbook 1915*). Some of the recipes used at Heritage Park are taken from cookbooks such as *Yesterday's Cook Book 1885, The Home Cook Book, First Edition 1877, The Blue Ribbon Cookbook 1905, Lowney's Cook Book 1907, Ogilvie's Book for a Cook 1914* and *The Prairie Wife's Cook Book, circa 1914.*

Pioneer families needed everyone to work. The children helped on the farm and in their homes in many ways. We have provided a few recipes and food-related rhymes children might enjoy in the Young Settlers section.

Heritage Park uses wood stoves in the programme for cooking and baking. We have included how to convert the temperature of the wood stoves for modern ovens.

The recipes in this book are historical by nature and sometimes the language used requires an explanation in modern terms. These explanations are shown in the recipes within *(brackets and italics)*.

We hope you enjoy this cookbook and invite you to visit us at Heritage Park to observe our Foodways Interpreters in action cooking in the Rectory, Burnside Ranch or Livingston Houses. When you do, be sure to ask them more about wood stove cooking in the early days.

Happy Cooking!

Barb Saunders, Foodways Lead Hand (retired)

INSTRUCTIONS FOR COOKING HISTORIC RECIPES

In order to get the same results that we get at the cooking sites in Heritage Park Historical Village you will need to use period ingredients: real butter, cream, and so on, when using these recipes. Historic recipes will not taste the same and may not work properly (and some may not work at all) when you substitute modern ingredients. These recipes were originally made using wood stoves. With no temperature indicators, oven temperatures were expressed as hot, slow, or very slow. Don't fret – we provide Fahrenheit equivalents so that you can cook them in a modern oven.

Some recipes lack details about how to combine ingredients because it was expected that everyone knew how to cook. The recipes in Wood Stove Cuisine are in their original historical form as a record of the past. Like the cooks in our Foodways Programme, you may need to experiment to get the best results.

MEASUREMENTS

Old recipes used different units of measurement than we do today. Standardized measurements did not appear until 1896. Where teaspoons or tablespoons are mentioned they are the spoons people ate or served with. A cup meant a teacup and a glass or tumbler was a small water glass. The following table gives the modern equivalents for the period measurements used in the recipes.

Liquids
4 quarts = 1 gallon
2 pints = 1 quart
2 (coffee) cups (ordinary tumblers) = 1 pint
1 tea cup = 1 cup or 8 ounces
1 tumbler = 1 cup or 8 ounces
1 tablespoon = 1/2 ounce
4 teaspoons = 1 tablespoon
Salt spoon = 1/4 teaspoon

Dry ingredients
4 cups flour = 1 pound or 1 quart
3 cups cornmeal = 1 pound
2 2/3 cups rolled oats or oatmeal = 1 pound
2 cups granulated sugar = 1 pound
2 2/3 cups brown sugar = 1 pound
2 1/2 cups powdered sugar = 1 pound
1 rounded tablespoon flour = 1/2 ounce, or one modern tablespoon

Miscellaneous
1 egg = 1 medium egg
10 eggs (or 9 large eggs) = 1 pound
A dash = 3 good shakes
1 tablespoon butter = 1 ounce
1 cup butter = 1/2 pound or 8 ounces
Butter the size of a hickory nut = 1 heaping teaspoon or 1/2 ounce
Butter the size of a walnut = 2 heaping teaspoons or 1 ounce
Butter the size of an egg = 1/3 cup or 2 ounces
Butter the size of a goose egg = 3/4 stick, 3/8 cup, or 3 ounces
1 package yeast = 2 teaspoons

OVEN TEMPERATURE CONVERSIONS

A 'very slow' oven has a temperature of approximately 250 degrees Fahrenheit and is often used for cooking meringues or dehydrating fruits, vegetables or meat.

A 'slow' oven has a temperature of approximately 300 degrees Fahrenheit and is often used for stews and casseroles.

A 'moderate' oven has a temperature of approximately 350 degrees Fahrenheit. Moderate is the most common temperature in cooking and is used for many dishes.

A 'hot' or quick oven has a temperature of approximately 400 degrees Fahrenheit. A hot oven is often used where a short cooking time is required or for browning such foods as biscuits or pies.

A 'very hot' oven has a temperature of approximately 450 degrees Fahrenheit.

Fahrenheit	Celsius	Description
225	107	Very Slow
250	121	
275	135	
300	149	Slow
325	163	
350	177	Moderate
375	191	Hot, or Quick
400	204	
425	218	
450	232	Very Hot
475	246	

HOW TO TELL THE TEMPERATURE
OF YOUR WOOD STOVE

If you put a tablespoon of flour on a baking tray and it turns brown in one minute in the oven — the temperature is moderate or about 350 to 375 degrees.

If you put your bare hand into the oven and can hold it comfortably for a count of 8 — the temperature is moderate. A count of 5 is a hot oven — over 400 degrees or hot enough to cook scones.

If you put a piece of writing paper in the oven and it curls up and browns — the temperature is just right for pastry.

To prevent salt from hardening in salt shakers, add a little corn starch when filling.

Laundry/work area, Livingston House

SAMPLE MENUS FROM EARLY WESTERN SETTLEMENT

Eating habits of the settlement period differed from our own. First courses were usually plain, bland and monotonous, often consisting of meat (boiled, fried, or roasted), potatoes and vegetables (boiled or baked). Desserts were the highlight of the meal and as long as the necessary ingredients were available, pies, puddings and cakes were to be expected. Foods were seasonal, which probably accounts for settlers' recollections of how good foods tasted in the "old days." The appearance of fresh garden produce or the first wild strawberries of the season provided such a welcome change that their memory of it likely was exaggerated.

1881

Supper: 'Potluck' served by Jane Livingston to the Marquis of Lorne — roast of freshly killed beef and venison, bacon rolls, corn on the cob, new potatoes, carrots and peas and cabbage salad. Dessert was Saskatoon berry pie.

July 1, 1882, Manitoba

Picnic: Cold sliced home-cured ham, lettuce cut up in sour cream, mustard and sugar, raisin buns, snail shell-shaped cinnamon rolls, doughnuts, ginger and molasses cookies, railroad cake, vinegar pies (because of a lack of both lemons and eggs), oranges, bananas (most present had never tasted a banana), chocolate-coated cream candy.

1893

Breakfast:	Oatmeal porridge, fat bacon, eggs, bread, butter, tea
Dinner:	Fat pork, potatoes and other vegetable, apple pie
Supper:	Rice & egg or canned salmon or hash, buttermilk pancakes and syrup

1910

Breakfast:	Bacon & egg, fried potatoes, prunes, syrup, bread & butter, coffee
Dinner:	Roast beef, gravy, potatoes, vegetable, pickles, bread & butter, tea
Supper:	Cold meat, potatoes or macaroni and cheese, stewed fruit, tea and milk

October 1912 Threshing

Breakfast:	Rolled oats porridge, eggs, cold boiled ham, potatoes, coffee, Sally Lunns (tea biscuits), stewed apples
Dinner:	Roast chicken, potatoes, cabbage, pickles, bread, butter, canned plums, cake, fresh milk and cream
Supper:	Ragout stew, fried potatoes, stewed carrots, tarts, apple pie, cooked fruit, tea, bread & butter, pickles

❖ ❖ ❖

Cleaning White Spots From the Icebox - The white spots appearing in the spring on the lining of your icebox will disappear if you rub the zinc with kerosene. Leave the icebox open several hours, then wash with water, soap and some ammonia. The icebox will then be clean and sweet, all spots will have disappeared.

❖ ❖ ❖

SOUPS

Soup is a primarily liquid food, generally served warm, that is made by combining ingredients such as meat and vegetables with stock, water or another liquid. It is often served as the starter or first course of a meal.

A chemist with the Campbell Soup Company invented condensed soup in 1897. Today, Campbell's Tomato, Cream of Mushroom, and Chicken Noodle Soup are three of the most popular soups in Canada.

Soups are similar to stews, and in some cases there may not be a clear distinction between the two, however, soups generally have more liquid than stews.

Pitcher for water or milk

LIVINGSTON HOUSE

Pea Soup

Soak the peas overnight. In the morning put them over the fire in cold water and parboil. Then throw off that water and pour boiling water over them. Add one medium-sized onion chopped and celery cut fine (if celery cannot be had, use celery seed tied in a fine piece of muslin). Boil constantly five

14

or six hours, stirring frequently to prevent burning. Season with pepper and salt just before serving and strain through a colander, mashing the peas. Boil in another kettle a piece of salt pork *(thick bacon)* and about ½ hour before serving add this to the soup. If the soup is too thick, add boiling water. Serve with pieces of pork cut fine and small squares of toasted or fired bread (optional).

Preserving and Fruit Canning Simplified, 1890

Note: Peas need not be soaked overnight. Use 1 cup peas to 6 cups water. The salt pork or bacon may be boiled in the same kettle as the peas.

Chicken Soup

Take 1 chicken *(we use a couple of chicken legs with backs attached)*, 4 quarts of water, 1 tablespoon of rice, 1 onion, 1 potato, 1 turnip, ½ cup tomatoes, 2 stalks of celery, salt and pepper. Boil the chicken, water and rice. Chop the potato, onion and turnip and add ½ hour after. Cut the celery in dice and add 20 minutes before serving. Add the tomato and seasoning last.

Dr. Chase's New Recipes, 1889

Barley Soup

Take a 2 – 3 lb piece of meat, ¼ lb of pearl barley, slice 2 small onions, chop 2 small carrots, 2 stalks of celery, salt and pepper. Put all into a soup kettle, cover with cold water and heat up slowly for an hour. Continue 3 – 4 more hours of more brisk boiling. Add celery and boil for 15 – 20 minutes.

Dr. Chase's New Recipes, 1889

Tomato Soup

One quart can of tomatoes; or twelve large ripe tomatoes, peeled and chopped; boil for an hour, then stir in a half teaspoon full of soda; when the foaming ceases add two soft crackers rolled very fine *(6 to 8 soup crackers may be used)*, one quart of milk, 1 tablespoonful of butter, salt and pepper to taste. Cook fifteen minutes. If too thick add milk or boiling water.

Yesterday's Cook Book, 1885

Tomato Soup and Tea Biscuits

Turnip peel washed clean and tied in a knot imparts a flavour to soup. Celery leaves and ends serve the same purpose.

RANCH HOUSE

Potato Soup

3 potatoes	4 cups milk
1 onion	2 stalks celery
1 teaspoon salt	pepper

Cook the potatoes in salt water with the onion. When soft, mash smooth and rub through a fine sieve. Scald the milk with the celery; add the butter and flour creamed together. Then add the prepared potatoes to the milk and season with salt and pepper. Let come to a boil and serve at once.

Ogilvie's Book for a Cook, 1914

Use a double boiler for scalding milk. When the water in the lower pan boils, the milk is scalded.

Velvet Soup

One quart of veal or chicken stock; and one-half cupful tapioca (soaked overnight), yolks of two eggs, salt and pepper to taste. Simmer the tapioca and stock. Beat egg yolks lightly with a little water. Put the eggs in the tureen, pour over them the soup, stirring all the while. Season with a few cloves, onion and carrot.

The High River Cook Book, 1907

Corn Chowder

4 cups potatoes, cut in ¼ inch slices
1 ½ inch cube fat salt pork (bacon)
1 can corn   4 cups scalded milk
1 sliced onion   salt and pepper

Cook pork in small pieces and fry out (render); add onions and cook five minutes, stirring often that onion may not burn; strain fat into a stew pan. Parboil potatoes five minutes in boiling water to cover; drain and add potatoes to fat; then add two cups boiling water; cook until potatoes are soft, add corn and milk, then heat to boiling point. Season with salt and pepper. Serve.

Circa 1914 (Heritage Park's Ranch House Cook Book)

Tomato Bisque Soup

1 can tomatoes   6 cloves (optional)
1 quart milk   1 ½ teaspoons salt
2 tbsps chopped onion   1 tsp chopped parsley
¼ cup flour   ¼ teaspoon soda
¼ cup butter   cayenne and celery salt

18

Melt butter, add onion, cook five minutes; add flour, milk and seasonings, cook in double boiler five minutes. Cook tomatoes, press through a sieve and add soda. Combine mixtures and strain. Serve immediately. If tomato is very acid, it may be necessary to add more soda to neutralize.

Lowney's Cook Book, 1907

Cream of Celery Soup

3 cups finely cut celery	3 tablespoons of butter
1 pint boiling water	¼ cup flour
2 ½ cups of milk	salt and pepper to taste
1 slice of onion	

Wash celery and cook in boiling water till soft, put through sieve, saving both water and celery. Scald milk with onion in it; remove onion at once; add milk to celery. Melt butter and add flour to butter; then add to celery and milk. Boil in double boiler until of the right consistency.

The High River Cook Book, 1907

RECTORY

Cookery For The Sick and Convalescent

According to the *Household Management Manual*, "the preservation of health is of far greater importance than to dose a man after he is sick". Good health depends on "regular occupation, abundant exercise, early hours and generous, but not imprudent diet". "Very weak patients must be rallied; stimulants may be necessary". Wine or brandy may be added to desserts or gruel.

19

Foods for the sick and convalescent should "provide the necessary nourishment and not strain any digestive organs that may be affected".

The food should be freshly prepared and daintily served and should include different dishes for each meal. Seasoning and flavouring should be used sparingly as the sense of taste may be abnormally sensitive.

Wash basin

Barley Gruel

Wash three heaping tablespoons of pearl barley; drop it into a pint of boiling water and par boil five minutes. Pour this water off and add a quart of fresh boiling water. Let it simmer gently for three hours; strain, season and serve. A small piece of lemon rind added to the gruel half an hour before it is done gives it a very agreeable flavour. Equal quantities of milk and barley gruel make a very nourishing drink. The milk however, should not be added to the gruel until needed, as in a warm atmosphere it undergoes quite a rapid change and is likely to ferment.

Preserving and Fruit Canning Simplified, 1890

To Soften Hands –
Cheap soap and
hard water are the
unknown enemies
of many people, and
the cause of rough
skin and chapped
hands. Castile soap
and rain water will
sometimes cure
without any other
assistance.

To Temper Glass –
Lamp chimneys and
glassware for hot
water are made less
liable to break by
putting in cold
water, bringing
slowly to boiling
point, boiling for an
hour and allowing
to cool before
removing from the
water.

❖ ❖ ❖

21

BREADS and BISCUITS

Breads and biscuits were a staple food in most meals. The test of a good cook was how good her breads or biscuits were. Single men who couldn't bake bread would buy it from women who did, or from the town bakery — if there was one.

Before the railroad was built, flour was scarce and was only available by I.G. Baker and Company bull trains from Fort Benton, Montana. As soon as possible, settlers grew enough grain for flour and seed. Purchased flour was available in ninety-eight pound bags usually referred to as 100 pound sacks. Settlers often bought enough to last a year, not only because of the difficulty in obtaining it, but also because aging improved the baking quality.

LIVINGSTON HOUSE

Buckskin Bread or Bannock

2 cups flour	1 teaspoon salt
1 teaspoon baking powder	1 cup water

Sift together dry ingredients. Quickly mix in water. Press the dough into a pie pan and bake in a hot oven *(400 degrees F)* for 25 minutes until lightly browned.

Aboriginal Recipe

Bannock was a Scottish food brought to Canada by Hudson Bay Traders and adopted by Aboriginal people. It can be baked, fried, deep-fried or roasted on a stick over a fire.

Corn Cake Without Eggs

One pint *(2 cups)* of sweet milk, 2 tablespoons of melted butter, 1 handful *(1/2 cup)* of flour and meal sufficient to make a batter *(2 ½ cups)*, 2 teaspoons of cream of tartar, 1 teaspoon of soda, 2 teaspoons of sugar. Bake in a hot oven *(400 degrees F)*.

Preserving and Fruit Canning Simplified, 1890

Note: The cream of tartar/soda combination was used at this time as a substitute for baking powder.

Tea Biscuits

One quart of sifted flour *(4 cups)*, a little salt, three teaspoonsful Royal baking powder, a small handful of sugar; mix lightly through the flour; rub a large tablespoonful of lard through the dry mixture; mix with water (it is better than milk), the colder the better; roll out soft to the thickness of about one-third of an inch; cut with a large-sized cutter and bake in a really hot oven *(425 to 450 degrees F)*.

Butter churn

Yesterday's Cook Book, 1885

Excellent Bread

One potato mashed fine, one teaspoon of salt, one pint *(2 cups)* of lukewarm milk, one-eighth cake of compressed yeast dissolved in one-eighth cup of warm water, flour enough to make a pliable dough, mould with hands well-greased with lard; place in pans and when sufficiently light *(risen)*, it is ready for baking.

Mrs. George Pitkin in The Home Cookbook, 1877

Note: This recipe is ¼ of the original. 1 cake yeast = one .25 ounce package of dry yeast. This recipe could be an alternative for the Corn Cake Without Eggs recipe.

RANCH HOUSE

Sage Bread

1 package active dry yeast	¼ cup warm water
¾ cup warm milk	2 tablespoons sugar
2 tablespoons shortening	2 teaspoons celery seed
1 ½ teaspoons salt	1 teaspoon sage
¼ teaspoon nutmeg	1 egg
3 cups flour	

Dissolve yeast in warm water. Add the milk, sugar, shortening, celery seed, salt, sage, nutmeg, egg and 2 cups flour. Beat until smooth. Stir in enough remaining flour to form a soft dough. Knead until smooth and elastic, about 5 minutes. Place in a well-greased bowl. Cover and let rise in a warm place until doubled (about 1 ¼ hours). Punch dough down. Shape into a round loaf. Place on a greased pie plate. Cover and let rise in a warm place until doubled (about 45 minutes). Bake in a hot oven *(400 degrees F)* for 35 to 40 minutes.

Circa 1914 (Dorothy Saunders – Everton, Ontario)

Sarah's Butter Biscuits – 1890

2 cups flour	3 tablespoons sugar
4 teaspoons baking powder	½ cup butter
½ teaspoon salt	¾ cup milk

Combine dry ingredients. Cut in butter until flakey. Quickly add milk, mixing until just moist. Pat out dough on floured board with palm of hand until ½ inch thick. Cut with biscuit cutter or knife. Bake in hot oven *(400 degrees F)* for 12 to 15 minutes.

The Pioneer Kitchens – 100ᵗʰ Anniversary, 1990

Bread Rolls

2 cups sifted flour	½ cup milk
1 tablespoon melted butter	1 teaspoon salt
2 teaspoons sugar	1 cake yeast

Dissolve the yeast in the milk. Add flour, sugar, salt and butter. Stir milk mixture into flour gradually. Give the dough a hard kneading, adding sufficient flour to make it soft. Cut dough and form into rolls. Place on buttered biscuit pans, set in a warm place to rise. Bake. *(400 degrees F)*

Circa 1914 (Dorothy Saunders – Everton, Ontario)

Note: 1 cake yeast = .25 ounce package of dry yeast

Rolls brushed with milk just before baking will have a brown crust. Rubbing the crust with butter just before it is taken from the oven will make it crisp.

Cinnamon Buns

Put *(cut)* ½ cup butter into 1 pint *(2 cups)* of flour; add ½ teaspoon salt, 4 teaspoons baking powder, (scant) 1 cup milk. Roll onto large tin sheet, spread with soft butter and sprinkle with sugar and cinnamon. Roll out *(up)* and cut into buns and bake 20 minutes in a hot oven *(400 degrees F)*.

Cinnamon Buns

Note: (scant) 1 cup milk is the measurement description. It refers to the amount of milk as being slightly short of the amount indicated.

Magnet Users Cookbook, 1915

26

Baking Powder Biscuits

2 cups sifted flour
2 tbsps butter or lard
1 teaspoon salt
4 teaspoons baking powder

1 tablespoon lard
¾ to 1 cup milk (half milk
& half water)

Mix and sift the dry ingredients. Add shortening and chop with knife (cut in with two knives) until mealy, add milk gradually until a soft spongy dough. Turn onto a floured board, toss with knife until whole surface is floured. Pat lightly with rolling pin until ½ inch thick. Cut in rounds and bake immediately on buttered sheet in quick oven *(400 degrees F)*.

Lowney's Cook Book, 1907

Corn Muffins

1 cup corn meal
1 cup flour
¼ cup sugar
1 cup milk

¼ cup butter
4 teaspoons baking powder
½ teaspoon salt
2 eggs

Cream butter; add sugar, yolks well beaten, flour mixed and sifted with corn meal, baking powder and salt, milk and beaten whites. Bake in buttered muffin tin 25 minutes in hot oven *(400 degrees F)*. A very good muffin may be made by using 2 tablespoons of butter and 1 egg.

Lowney's Cook Book, 1907

28

MAIN DISHES

For people living on farms and ranches, the main meal was at midday and it was called dinner. Supper was a smaller meal at the end of the day.

When they moved onto their land, settlers planted potatoes right away. Potatoes were often eaten two or three times a day. Other root vegetables including beets, carrots, onions and parsnips were grown successfully and stored well in winter. Lettuce, peas and beans were common. Corn, cucumbers and tomatoes were not grown before 1910

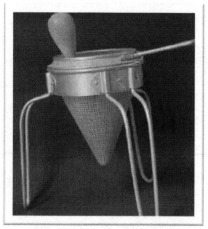

Beacon Ware colander/strainer

because of June frost. Canned corn and canned tomatoes were available in stores or by mail order from the late 1800's.

For the first year or two, newly arrived settlers depended on wild game. On the plains, rabbit was a staple in both summer and winter. Ducks, geese, partridge and prairie chickens were seasonal. For settlers living near lakes or rivers, fish was important. Cattle, pigs, and chickens were not obtained until two or more years after settling, but once they arrived, they provided milk, eggs and meat.

29

Sausages with Tomatoes

Tomatoes and sausages are capital. Fry the sausages and arrange them in a dish in front of the fire. Cut the tomatoes into slices with some onions thinly sliced; fry them, season them with pepper and salt, place them among the sausages, and serve hot.

Sausage with Tomatoes and Scalloped Potatoes

Yesterday's Cook Book, 1885

Scalloped Potatoes (Southern Style)

Peel and slice raw potatoes thin, the same as for frying. Butter an earthen dish, put in a layer of potatoes and season with salt, pepper, butter, a bit of onion chopped fine, if liked; sprinkle a little flour over all. Now put another layer of potatoes and seasonings. Continue in this way till the dish is filled. Just before putting into the oven, pour a quart of hot milk over. Bake three quarters of an hour.

Cold boiled potatoes may be cooked the same. It requires less time to bake them. They are delicious either way. If the onion is disliked, it can be omitted.

Preserving and Fruit Canning Simplified, 1890

When the sauce bubbles through the crumbs on top of a scallop dish, the cooking is complete.

Beets

Clean these nicely, but do not pare them, leaving on a short piece of the stalk. Then put over to boil in hot water. Young beets will cook tender in an hour; old beets require several hours boiling. When done, skin quickly while hot, slice thin into your vegetable dish. Put salt, pepper and a little butter; put a little vinegar over and serve hot or cold.

The Home Cook Book, 1877

Cole Slaw

Select a fine bleached cabbage, cut up enough into shreds to fill a large salad bowl or according to the quantity required. Shave very fine and after that chop up, the more thoroughly the better. Put this into a dish in which it is to be served, after seasoning it well with salt and pepper. Turn over it a dressing for coleslaw as given, mix it well and garnish with slices of hard boiled eggs.

Dressing for Cole Slaw

Beat well two eggs and two tablespoons full of sugar; add a piece of butter the size of an egg *(2 tablespoons)*, a teaspoon full of mustard, a little pepper and then add a teacup of vinegar. Put all these ingredients into a dish over the fire and cook like soft custard, but using less vinegar.

Preserving and Fruit Canning Simplified, 1890

RANCH HOUSE

Salmon Loaf

One can of salmon, 4 eggs beaten, butter the size of an egg *(2 tablespoons),* five soda biscuits rolled fine, pepper and salt. Bake in a moderate oven *(350 degrees F)* half an hour. Serve with white sauce.

Magnet Users Cook Book, Circa 1915

Note: Use 2 regular cans of salmon. Bake until a knife inserted in the centre comes out clean. Loaf should be nicely puffed.

White Sauce

2 tablespoons butter	¼ teaspoon salt
2 tablespoons flour	few grains cayenne
1 cup milk	¼ teaspoon pepper

Melt butter; add flour, seasonings and liquid. Stir until boiling point is reached. Boil five minutes, beating constantly.

Lowney's Cook Book, 1907

Scalloped Tomatoes

Arrange in layers canned tomatoes and bread cut in cubes; sprinkle each layer with salt and pepper, dot with butter. Bake one half hour. For variety, rub dish with onion before putting in tomato.

Lowney's Cook Book, 1907

Beefsteak Pie

2 lbs round steak cut ¼ inch thick	Pepper
	1 onion sliced
1 heaping tablespoon flour	2 tablespoons butter
2 medium potatoes sliced thin	1 teaspoon salt

Beefsteak Pie

Cut the steak into strips 1 ½ inch long and 1 inch wide. Place in a saucepan, cover with boiling water, add the sliced onion and simmer until the meat is tender. Remove the meat, discard onion, add potatoes to the liquid and parboil six minutes then remove the potatoes. Measure the liquid and add enough boiling water to make one pint, add the seasonings. Cream the butter and flour together, add to the liquid and cook 5 minutes.

In the bottom of a pudding dish, place a layer of one-half the potatoes and on top of this arrange the meat, placing the other half of the potatoes on top of it. Pour over this sufficient gravy to entirely cover the contents of the baking dish. When cool, cover with a crust and bake in a hot oven *(400 degrees F)*.

Ogilvie's Book for a Cook, 1914

Crust for Beefsteak Pie

1 cup flour	1 tablespoon butter
1 tablespoon lard	½ teaspoon salt
1 teaspoon baking power	

Sift flour, baking powder and salt. Cream butter and lard together and combine them with the dry ingredients, mixing thoroughly with finger tips. Add enough milk to make soft dough, roll out about ½ inch thick and cover with it, the contents of the pudding dish.

Ogilvie's Book for a Cook, 1914

Chicken and Dumplings

4 lbs stewing chicken, water to cover

1 medium onion sliced	½ cup heavy cream
2 stalks of celery and leaves	1 teaspoon salt
1 bay leaf	1 teaspoon sage
6 tablespoons flour	½ teaspoon thyme
1/8 teaspoon pepper	

Cut the chicken in serving pieces and place in a large pot, cover chicken with water. Add the onions, celery and the bay leaf. Cover and simmer for 3 hours or until tender. Remove chicken, strain and measure broth. There should be 4 cups of broth. If more, reduce by boiling; if less, add more water. Mix flour and a little cold water to form a smooth paste. Stir into broth and heat until thickened. Add cream, salt, sage, thyme and pepper. Remove the chicken from bones and return meat to gravy.

For the Dumplings

1 egg	1 ½ cups flour
1 cup milk	2 teaspoons baking powder
½ teaspoon salt	

Sift flour, baking powder and salt into a bowl. Mix egg and milk and stir into the dry ingredients. Drop into the hot gravy and simmer covered for 20 minutes. Do not lift lid until time is up.

Circa 1914 (Heritage Park's Ranch House Cook Book)

Macaroni Cheese with Tomatoes

Pour the contents of a package of macaroni into boiling salted water as per directions, when cooked drain and put into saucepan with one can tomatoes, let simmer a few minutes, then add a cup or more grated cheese and butter the size of two eggs *(4 tablespoons)*. Let simmer for another five minutes. Pepper well and serve.

Magnet Users Cook Book, circa 1915

Egg Sandwiches

Hard boil some fresh eggs and when cold, cut them into moderately thin slices and lay them between some bread and butter, cut as thin as possible. Season them with pepper, salt and nutmeg. For picnic parties or when one is traveling, these sandwiches are far preferable to hard-boiled eggs *au naturel.*

The White House Cook Book, 1898

Cut bread for fancy sandwiches lengthwise instead of across the loaf and there is less waste.

Egg beater

PUDDINGS, PIES and TARTS

Housewives tried to provide variety with puddings, pies and tarts. A whole week's supply of pies was often baked on Saturday and stored in a pie safe or cupboard made with panels of pierced tin which let air flow through but kept flies and other bugs out. During the first years on a homestead, puddings, dumplings and pie were generally made with flour, suet, water, dried fruits, and spices such as cinnamon, ginger, nutmeg, and cloves. Eggs and milk were scarce and sugar, if available, was expensive. Molasses was used as a sugar substitute to sweeten desserts.

LIVINGSTON HOUSE

Cottage Pudding

Two cups of flour, one of sugar, one and a half cups of milk, two tablespoons butter, one or two eggs, one teaspoonful of cream of tartar and soda. Flavour with vanilla; bake in moderate oven *(350 degrees F)*; serve with cream or sauce.

The Home Cook Book, 1877

Rice Pudding without Eggs

Two quarts of milk, half a teacup of rice, a little less than a teacup of sugar, the same quantity of raisins, a teaspoon of cinnamon or allspice (a little nutmeg and salt). Wash the rice and put it with the rest of the ingredients into the milk; put into a deep pudding dish, well buttered; bake rather slowly

(250 – 300 degrees F) from two to three hours; stir two or three times the first hour of baking. If properly done, this pudding is delicious.

The Home Cook Book, 1877

RANCH HOUSE

Cottage Pudding

1 cup sugar
¼ cup butter
2 eggs
¼ teaspoon salt

1 cup milk
2 cups flour
3 teaspoons baking powder

Cream butter and sugar, add yolks of eggs beaten until thick, flour in which baking powder and salt have been sifted, alternately with milk, beat well and add well beaten whites. Pour into a well buttered pudding dish. Bake forty-five minutes *(350 degrees F)*. Serve with vanilla or white sauce.

Lowney's Cook Book, 1907

Caramel Pudding

1 quart milk *(4 cups)*
2 tablespoons corn starch
1 egg
Vanilla

1 cup brown sugar
pinch of salt
small piece of butter
heavy cream

Put butter and brown sugar in a pan to brown. In another pan heat the milk and when hot add the cornstarch dissolved in a little cold water. Add the brown sugar and the egg. Cook until thick and set aside to cool. Serve with cream.

Five Roses Flour Cook Book, 1913

Brown Betty

One cup of breadcrumbs, two cups chopped tart apples, half a cup of sugar, one teaspoon of cinnamon and two teaspoons of butter cut into small pieces. Butter a deep dish and put a layer of chopped apples at the bottom, sprinkle with sugar, a few bits of butter and cinnamon, cover with bread crumbs then more apples. Proceed in this order until the dish is full, having layer of breadcrumbs at the top. Cover closely and steam three quarters of an hour in a moderate oven *(350 degrees F)*. Then uncover and brown quickly. Eat warm with sugar and cream or sweet sauce. Serve in the dish in which it is baked.

Twentieth Century Home Cook Book, 1906

Brown Betty and ice cream

Pie – Puff Paste (Fine)

To make fine puff paste take one pound *(4 cups)* flour, half a pound *(1 cup)* of butter and half a pound *(1 cup)* of lard *(we use shortening instead of lard)*. Cut the butter and lard in thin pieces through the cold sifted flour. Mix the whole with enough ice water to make it roll easily. There must be no kneading and the warm hands should come in contact with dough as little as possible.

Twentieth Century Home Cook Book, 1906

Note: The use of the word "paste" means pastry. The above recipe makes enough pastry for TWO double crust pies.

Mock Apple Pie

Crush finely with a rolling pin, one large Boston cracker *(about 1 ½ sleeves soda crackers)*, put it into a bowl and pour upon it one teacup of cold water. Add one teacup of white sugar, the juice and pulp of one lemon, half a lemon rind grated an a little nutmeg. Line the pie plate with half puff paste and bake half an hour. These proportions are for one pie.

The White House Cook Book, 1898

Rhubarb Pie

Prepare the stalks by peeling off the thin, reddish skin and cutting in half or three quarter inch pieces, which spread evenly in your crust lined tins. Sift on a little flour, to which add a bit of butter and a teacup of sugar, if for a large pie. However, when it is desirable to economize sugar or when a very sharp sour taste not relished, a pinch of soda may be used to advantage with less sugar, as it goes far to neutralizing the acid. If you live in a new country without fruit, raise a good patch of rhubarb, save all your surplus, prepare as for use and dry in the sun, as stove heat turns it dark coloured. Soak a stew for winter use, with sugar and soda as for above pies. It makes a nice sauce for tea. All tart fruit pies may be made in the same manner as directed for rhubarb pies. Simply varying the proportions of sugar according to the fruit and omitting the flour.

Twentieth Century Home Cook Book, 1906

Raisin Pie

One-half pound raisins (stoned). Pour over them 1 ½ cups boiling water, let boil for five or ten minutes. 1 small cup sugar, 1 teaspoon butter. Thicken with 1 teaspoon cornstarch wet with cold water, let come to a boil. Bake with two crusts in a quick oven *(400 degrees F)*.

Magnet Users Cook Book, circa 1915

RECTORY

Butter Tarts

1 egg	1 cup sugar
1 cup currants	3 tablespoons cream
1 teaspoon vanilla	1 tablespoon butter

Magnet Users Cook Book, circa 1915

Note: Use half the recipe for Puff Paste

CAKES

Cake was not only a dish for the wealthy. Everyone ate cake.

When making most cakes, especially sponge cake, the flour should be added by degrees, stirred very slowly and lightly, for if stirred hard and fast it will make it porous and tough.

The White House Cook Book, 1898

LIVINGSTON HOUSE

Coffee Cake

1 cup butter, 1 cup sugar, 1 cup molasses, 1 cup cold coffee, 4 cups flour with 2 teaspoons baking powder, ½ pound raisins, ¼ pound citron, 1 teaspoon each of nutmeg, cinnamon and cloves.

Dr. Chase's New Recipes, 1889

Good Plain Cake

2 eggs, butter the size of an egg, 1 cup sugar, ½ cup sweet milk, ½ teaspoon soda, 1 teaspoon cream of tartar, 2 cups flour.

Dr. Chase's New Recipes, 1889

White Sponge Cake

1 cup sugar, 1 cup flour, whites of ten eggs, 1 teacup coconut, 1 teaspoon cream of tartar in the flour.

Dr. Chase's New Recipes, 1889

RANCH HOUSE

Burnt Sugar Cake

Put in a dish one small cup granulated sugar, let melt and brown until a dark brown, then pour into it 1½ cups hot water, stirring until sugar is dissolved. Set aside to cool. Cream together 1 cup sugar and ½ cup butter (scant). Add 3 eggs well beaten, 2/3 cup burnt sugar water and 1/3 cup of sweet milk. Flavour with vanilla (No other flavour will do nor is it good without). Add flour for proper consistency for cake and 1 ½ teaspoons baking powder.

Note: The remainder of the burnt sugar water was to have been used in the recipe for icing, which we found was a failure. Therefore, only half the amount of burnt sugar water needs to be made. Ice the cake with butter icing.

Butter Icing

Beat 2 ½ tablespoons butter to a cream; add two small cups icing sugar, 1 ½ teaspoons vanilla, sprinkle with minced walnuts (optional).

Both recipes from Magnet Users Cook Book, 1915

A little flour dredged over the top of a cake before the icing is put on will keep the icing from running.

Marble cake

½ cup butter	½ teaspoon cinnamon
1 cup sugar	½ teaspoon nutmeg
2 egg yolks	¼ teaspoon salt
½ cup milk	1 ¾ cups flour
2 egg whites	3 teaspoons baking powder
1 tablespoon molasses	

Cream butter; add sugar, yolks of eggs beaten until thick, flour in which baking powder has been sifted, alternately with milk and egg whites, beaten stiff. To one third of this mixture add the spices. Pour into pan the light and dark mixtures irregularly.

Lowney's Cook Book, 1907

Note: The molasses is added to one third of the mixture along with the spices. After pouring light and dark mixtures into pan, swirl with a knife. Ice the cake with butter icing.

A dash of salt added to the whites of eggs makes them whip better.

Marble Cake

Edith's Mahogany Cake

½ cup grated chocolate, ½ cup sweet milk, cooked together until thick. 1 ½ cups sugar, ½ cup butter, 3 eggs. Beat well all ingredients. Add ½ cup sweet milk, 1 teaspoon soda, 2 teaspoons vanilla, 2 cups flour.

Magnet Users Cook Book, 1915

RECTORY

Cocoa cake

½ cup butter
1 ½ cups sugar
4 eggs
½ cup cocoa
1 teaspoon vanilla

½ cup milk
1 ½ cups flour
2 teaspoons baking powder
¼ teaspoon salt

Mix in the order given and beat well for five minutes. Bake in buttered pan thirty to forty minutes in moderate oven *(350 degrees F)*.

Lowney's Cook Book, 1907

Raspberry Cake

Two eggs, three quarters of a cup of sugar, one-half cup of butter, two small cups of flour, one teaspoonful of soda dissolved in a tablespoonful of hot milk, one cup of canned raspberries. This makes two layers. Oven should not be too hot *(325 – 350 degrees F)*.

High River Cook Book, 1907

King Edward Cake

1 ½ cups butter	1 teaspoon cinnamon
2 eggs	1 tablespoon molasses
½ teaspoon nutmeg	(heaping)
1 cup raisins seeded	½ cup sour milk
1 teaspoon soda	2 small cups flour
1 cup brown sugar	

Bake in a moderate oven *(350 degrees F)*. Ice the cake with icing.

Magnet Users Cook Book, 1915

Notes: To sour milk, add 2 teaspoons vinegar to it. Let stand at room temperature until curdled. Remove 2 teaspoons of milk before adding other ingredients.
Suggested amount of flour is 1¾ cups.

Date Squares

1 lb pitted dates	¾ cup sugar
1 cup water	pinch salt
1 tsp vanilla	2 cups oatmeal
1 ½ cups flour	¼ tsp salt
1 tsp baking soda	1 cup brown sugar
⅔ cup butter	

For the filling, put dates into saucepan on hot stove. Cover with water. Add sugar and pinch of salt. Cook until thick, stir often. Remove from heat, stir in vanilla. For the crumbs, put oatmeal, flour, ¼ tsp salt, baking soda, brown sugar and butter into a bowl. Rub altogether to make crumbs. Grease square pan. Add ½ crumbs and pat down. Spread filling carefully and evenly. Add rest of crumbs and pat gently. Bake for 20 minutes, or until golden brown.

Circa 1914 (Heritage Park's Rectory Cook Book)

Preserving Oil Cloth – If oil cloth be occasionally rubbed with a mixture of beeswax and turpentine, it will last longer.

COOKIES

Cookies were not a daily treat, but were served at ladies social gatherings and during visits with local clergy at the Rectory or Manse.

Cookie varieties were divided into five basic types: bar, drop, icebox, roll, and shaped, each determined by the consistency of the dough and how it is formed into cookies.

For even baking and browning of cookies, bake them in the center of the oven. If the heat distribution in your oven is uneven, turn the cookie sheet halfway through the baking time. Most cookies bake quickly and should be watched carefully to make sure they don't burn.

LIVINGSTON HOUSE

Ginger Snaps

¾ cup shortening	Granulated sugar
1 egg	1 cup brown sugar
2 ¼ cups flour	¼ cup molasses
1 teaspoon cinnamon	2 teaspoons soda
½ teaspoon cloves	1 teaspoon ginger
(ground)	¼ teaspoon salt

Thoroughly mix shortening, brown sugar, egg and ½ molasses. Blend in remaining ingredients except granulated sugar. Cover and let stand for 1 hour.

Shape dough by rounded teaspoonfuls into balls. Dip tops in granulated sugar. Place balls sugared side up 3 inches apart on lightly greased baking sheet. Bake (*350 degrees F for 10 to 12 minutes*) just until set. Immediately remove from baking sheet.

Circa 1880 (Heritage Park Livingston House Cook Book)

RANCH HOUSE

Shortbread

½ cup cornstarch	½ cup icing sugar
1 cup flour	¾ cup butter

Sift together cornstarch, icing sugar and flour. With wooden spoon, blend in butter until soft smooth dough forms. Shape into 1-inch balls. (*If dough is too soft to handle, cover and chill 30 to 60 minutes.*) Place 1½ inches apart on a greased cookie sheet. Flatten with lightly floured fork. Bake in moderate oven (*350 degrees F*) for 15 to 20 minutes until edges are lightly browned.

Circa 1914 (Heritage Park Ranch House Cook Book)

To Prevent Moths – Wet a piece of cloth in oil of cedar and lay in drawers.

Pinwheel Cookies

1 cup butter	1 cup sugar
1 egg	3 cups flour
3 teaspoons baking powder	1 teaspoon vanilla
6 tablespoons milk	2 squares chocolate

Cream butter and sugar. Add egg. Mix flour and baking powder and add alternately with milk. Add vanilla. Divide dough in 2 parts, adding melted chocolate to 1 part. Roll each separately into oblong sheets and place one on top of the other. Roll tightly and cool until firm. Slice and bake.

Circa 1914 (Heritage Park Ranch House Cook Book)

Icebox Cookies

1 cup butter	2 teaspoons baking powder
2 cups brown sugar	½ cups raisins
2 eggs	1 teaspoon vanilla
3 ½ cups flour	

Cream butter and sugar; add eggs well beaten. Sift flour with baking powder and add to butter and sugar. Add vanilla and raisins. Form into a long roll about 2 inches in diameter; wrap in waxed paper and let stand in the icebox until stiff enough to cut off in thin slices. Bake in a moderate oven (*350 degrees F*).

The Prairie Wife's Cook Book, circa 1914

❖ ❖ ❖

Removing Ink Spots From Wash Goods – Rub goods with yolk of an egg before washing.

❖ ❖ ❖

Jim Jams

1 cup butter
1 cup brown sugar, packed
6 tablespoons corn syrup
2 eggs

2 ½ cups flour
1 ½ teaspoons baking soda
apricot jam

Cream butter, brown sugar and corn syrup together. Beat in eggs. Fold in dry ingredients. Roll out thinly on lightly floured board and cut into 2 inch circles. Place on ungreased baking sheet. Bake about 8 minutes. Put together with jam. These become softer with age and are very tasty.

Circa 1914 (Heritage Park Ranch House Cook Book)

Jim Jams

Chocolate Cookies

½ cup butter

1 cup sugar

1 teaspoon cinnamon

½ teaspoon soda

2 ½ cups flour

1 tablespoon lard

(shortening)

¼ teaspoon salt

1 egg

2 tablespoons milk

2 oz. unsweetened

chocolate (melted)

Beat to a cream the butter and lard, gradually beat into this the sugar then add the salt, cinnamon and chocolate. Now add the well-beaten egg and the soda dissolved in the milk. Stir in enough flour to make soft dough, cut in round cakes and bake in a quick oven (*400 degrees F*).

The secret of making good cookies is in the use of as little flour as will suffice.

Ogilvie's Book for a Cook, 1914

Sugar Cookies

¾ cup shortening

1 cup butter

2 ½ cups flour

1 teaspoon salt

2 eggs

1 teaspoon vanilla

1 teaspoon baking powder

Mix thoroughly, shortening, butter, sugar, eggs and vanilla. Blend in flour, baking powder and salt. Roll dough 1/8 inch thick. Place cookies on ungreased sheet. Bake. (*350 degrees F*)

Circa 1914 (Heritage Park Rectory Cook Book)

53

Hermits

¾ cup butter
1 cup brown sugar
2 eggs
¾ teaspoon soda
¼ teaspoon each, cloves,
mace, nutmeg

2 ½ cups of flour
½ teaspoon salt
1 teaspoon cinnamon
1 cup raisins

Mix ingredients in order given. Roll mixture ¼ inch thick. Shape with cookie cutter. Put one raisin in centre of each round. Bake in moderate oven (*350 degrees F*) twelve to fifteen minutes.

Lowney's Cook Book, 1907

Snickerdoodles

1 cup butter and
shortening (½ & ½)
1 ½ cup sugar
2 eggs
2 ¾ cups flour

2 teaspoons cream of tartar
1 teaspoon soda
¼ teaspoon salt
½ cup granulated sugar
1 teaspoon cinnamon

Cream butter, shortening and sugar together. Add other ingredients, except second sugar amount and cinnamon, and mix well. Roll in balls and roll in a sugar and cinnamon mixture. Place on a lightly greased cookie sheet. Bake in a hot oven (*375 to 400 degrees F*) about 8 to 10 minutes.

Circa 1914 (Heritage Park Rectory Cook Book)

Coconut Macaroons

Whites of 3 eggs (beaten stiff)

Mix 1 cup of sugar and 1 teaspoon cornstarch. Add to whites. Stir over boiling water for 10 minutes (*double boiler*). Add about 1 ½ cups of coconut. Drop on buttered paper (*parchment*) and bake about 10 minutes in a moderate oven (*350 degrees F*)

The Prairie Wife's Cook Book, circa 1914

Colander

YOUNG SETTLERS

Pioneer families needed their children to work. The children helped on the farm and in their homes in many ways.

Girls helped with the cooking, cleaning, sewing, and taking care of the younger children.

Boys fetched wood and water, helped with the planting and harvesting of crops and also helped hunt for food to feed the family.

Their chores were often so time consuming that they were kept home from school in order to complete the work. But chores were both *necessary and educational*. Working alongside their parents, boys and girls learned many skills they would need later to run a farm and to raise a family.

LIVINGSTON HOUSE

Molasses Candy

Two cups of molasses; one of sugar; one tablespoon of vinegar; a piece of butter size of a walnut. Boil briskly and constantly for twenty minutes, stirring all the time. When cool enough, pull it quickly till it is white.

Preserving & Fruit Canning Simplified, 1890

RANCH HOUSE

Plain Ice Cream

4 cups milk	3 eggs
1 cup sugar	1 tablespoon vanilla
1/8 teaspoon salt	

Beat eggs very light, whip them with sugar, heat milk and stir into the eggs and sugar a little at a time, mixing well. Place on stove and heat until it thickens, stirring all the time. Remove from stove and set aside to cool. When cool, freeze.

This is the simplest and cheapest ice cream made. Place custard in ice cream maker and add one pint of cream. Crank ice cream maker until ice cream forms.

Lowney's Cook Book, 1907/ Preserving & Fruit Canning Simplified, 1890

Marshmallow Candy

One level tablespoon gelatine, 1 level tablespoon cold water, 7 level tablespoons hot water, 1 ½ cups granulated sugar, 1 teaspoon vanilla. Beat to a cream. Put on a flat dish, cut in squares, roll in icing sugar.

Magnet Users Cook Book, 1915

RECTORY

Breakfast Cocoa

2 tablespoons Cocoa	1 cup boiling water
2 tablespoons sugar	1/8 teaspoon salt

Mix cocoa, sugar and salt, add one cup boiling water gradually, when smooth boil five minutes. Add two cups scalded milk, beat with eggbeater until frothy.

Lowney's Cook Book, 1907

Lemonade

Boil two cups of sugar and four cups of water until a rich syrup is formed. Add one cup lemon juice. Dilute with ice water.

Lowney's Cook Book, 1907

Lemonade

FOOD RELATED SONGS AND RHYMES

Pease Porridge

Pease porridge hot
Pease porridge cold
Pease porridge in the pot
Nine days old

Some like it hot
Some like it cold
I like it in the pot
Nine days old

Chick, Chick, Chick, Chick, Chicken

Chick, chick, chick, chick, chicken,
Lay a little egg for me.
Chick, chick, chick, chick, chicken,
I want one for my tea.
I haven't had an egg since Easter,
And now it's half past three.
So, chick, chick, chick, chicken,
Lay a little egg for me.

Pancake Song

Mix a pancake,
Beat a pancake,
Put it in a pan.
Cook a pancake,
Toss a pancake,
Catch it if you can.

Pea Soup

(Hold one hand up with all five fingers extended)

One little pea,
Jumped into the pot,
And waited for the soup to get hot.
(Tuck thumb into fist)

Two little peas jumped into the pot,
And waited for the soup to get hot.
(Tuck pointer finger into fist)

Three little peas jumped into the pot,
And waited for the soup to get hot.
(Tuck middle finger into fist)

Four little peas jumped into the pot,
And waited for the soup to get hot.
(Tuck ring finger into fist)

Four little peas jumped into the pot,
And waited for the soup to get hot.
(Tuck little finger into fist)

Finally the soup got so very hot,
All the little peas jumped out of the pot!
(Open hand and wiggle all your fingers)

Jelly on the Plate

Jelly on the plate,
Jelly on the plate.
Wibble, wobble, wibble, wobble,
Jelly on the plate.

Hot Cross Buns

Hot cross buns!
Hot cross buns!
One a penny, two a penny.
Hot cross buns!

If you have no daughters,
Give them to your sons!
One a penny, two a penny.
Hot cross buns!

Heritage Park summer campers with Bart the Donkey

HISTORICAL FOOD INFORMATION

ARTICLES REQUIRED FOR THE KITCHEN

The following list will show what articles are necessary for the kitchen and will be quite an aid to young housekeepers when about commencing to furnish the utensils needed in the kitchen department and may prove useful to many.

1 Sweeping broom and dust pan	1 Whisk broom
1 Bread box	1 Colander
1 Egg beater	2 Scoops 1 for flour and 1 for sugar
1 Large flour box	1 Flour sifter
1 Jelly mould	1 Large-sized tin pepper box
1 Can opener	1 Spice box containing smaller spice boxes
2 Cake pans, two sizes	4 Bread pans
4 Stone jars	1 Coffee mill
3 Wooden spoons	1 Chopping-knife
2 Wooden chopping bowls, two sizes	1 Wire toaster
1 Double boiler	1 Tin steamer
1 Meat saw	1 Apple corer
1 Lemon squeezer	2 Large earthen bowls
1 Set of tin measures	2 Dippers, two sizes
1 Clothes wringer	4 Flat irons, 2#8 and 2#6
1 Ash bucket	1 Coal shovel
1 Wooden butter bowl	1 Wooden butter ladle
1 Tea canister	1 Tea kettle
1 Waffle iron	1 Bean pot
4 Pie pans	1 Set jelly cake tins
1 Coffee canister	2 Frying pans, two sizes
2 Granite ware stew pans	1 Tin or granite ware coffee pot

1 Pair scales	1 Griddle cake turner, also 1 griddle
1 Kitchen table	1 Stove
1 Wash boiler	2 Kitchen chairs
1 Large clothes basket	1 Wash board
1 Clothes wringer	8 Dozen clothes pins
1 Milk strainer	4 Milk pans

The White House Cook Book, 1898

THE HIGH COST OF GROCERIES

A shopping list in the 1880's would have included sugar, tea, flour, dried apples, baking soda, salt, oatmeal, rice syrup and perhaps coffee. In remote areas, shopping trips may only have been made once or twice a year, usually in the spring and fall.

Basic foodstuffs

1880's Tea – 35 cents/pound,
      Molasses - $5.00/5 pound wooden pail

1884 Yellow or brown sugar (if available) - $2.25/10 pound sack

1889 Flour (2nd grade) - $2.00/98 pound sack

Early 1900's
      Snowflake Baking Powder – 10 cents/pound tin
      Soda biscuits – 8 cents/pound
      St. Lawrence Corn Starch – 8 cents/package
      Beans – 10 cents/3 pounds
      Bakers Cocoa – 27 cents/1/2 pound tin
      Cheddar cheese – 15 cents/pound
      Jamaica coffee – 25 cents/pound
      White sugar – 1.00/20 pound

China black tea – 20 cents/pound
Yeast cakes – 4 cents/package
Lard – 35 cents/pound
Icing sugar – 7 cents/pound
Butter – 15 to 25 cents/pound

Product and Brand Name History

The following list is drawn from several secondary sources and because dates have not been verified against primary sources, it should be used as a general guide only. It is important to note that not all products were universally, available at the same time. Differences in availability are also likely to have existed between rural and urban centres. (Much of the following information provided by Tom Reitz, Manager/Curator, Doon Heritage Crossroads, Kitchener Ontario)

1835   Lea & Perrins Worcestershire Sauce

1884   Eaton's mail order service begins filling orders

Pre-1890   Soap: Sunlight and Fels Naptha

1890   Syrup: Beehive and Rogers, available in 5 or 10 pound tins
            Tea: Red Rose and Blue Ribbon
            Flour: Ogilvie's, Five Roses and Purity

1896   Heinz "57 Varieties"

1897   Cadbury's Milk Chocolate
            Grape Nut (C.W. Post, Battle Creek, Michigan)
            Jell-O (Leroy, New York)

1898	Graham Crackers (National Biscuit Company, USA)
1899	Bassett's Licorice All-Sorts Social Tea Biscuits (National Biscuit Company, USA)
1900	Toblerone Chocolate Bar (Switzerland) Johnson & Johnson baby care products OXO liquid
1902	Barnum's Animal Crackers (National Biscuit Company, USA)
1903	Perrier (French table water started by an Englishman)
1904	Ovaltine Canada Dry Pale Ginger Ale Dr. Scholl's Arch Supports
1905	Hershey Chocolate Bars Old Dutch Cleanser Brasso
1906	Kellogg's Toasted Corn Fakes
1908	Colgate's Ribbon Dental Cream
1909	Max Factor Perfume and Make-up (Missouri)
1910	OXO cubes
1911	Beech-Nut gum Crisco Shortening

| 1912 | American shaving cream tube (William Mennen) |
| | Oreo biscuits |

1913	Quaker Puffed Rice
	Brillo Steel Wool pads
	Camel and Chesterfield cigarettes
	Peppermint Life Savers

| 1914 | Fry's Turkish Delight bar |

| 1915 | "Classic" Coca-Cola Bottle shape |

ABOUT HERITAGE PARK HISTORICAL VILLAGE

In 1878, before the railway was completed, before Calgary was a town or Alberta was even a province, a man by the name of Sam Livingston stood on the land where Heritage Park now exists and was so taken with its beauty, he declared it his own. Sam settled the land with his wife, Jane and their 14 children.

Fast-forward 83 years. Sam's story, and existing home, were the inspiration for what was to become Heritage Park Historical Village. On July 1st, 1964 Heritage Park opened to 10,000 guests, anxious to get a glimpse into the past. At that time, the Park featured a handful of exhibits and an operating locomotive.

Today, Heritage Park has grown into Canada's largest living history experience, with over 180 exhibits and 50,000 artifacts. This museum connects visitors to the settlement of Western Canada from the 1860s to the 1950s by presenting the stories and lifestyles of people like Sam Livingston in an accurate and authentic manner.

Sam's log home is open to visitors, his garden is full of heirloom vegetables (which are used in Heritage Park's own kitchens), and the aroma of a hearty prairie meal is a welcoming smell from his wife Jane's kitchen.

BURNSIDE RANCH HOUSE

Built in 1904 at Grand Valley, 5 miles northwest of Cochrane, Alberta

Ewan Donald MacKay was born in Edinburgh, Scotland in 1838. Soon after the death of his wife in the late 1880s, MacKay and his son Alex immigrated to Canada. The two first settled in Calgary, but in 1900, the elder MacKay built himself a simple log cabin with a sod roof in Grand Valley, north of Cochrane. He named his homestead 'Burnside,' an old English term for 'beside the creek.'

Burnside Ranch House

Alex MacKay eventually joined his father and together they raised and trained registered Clydesdale horses. In 1904, Ewan MacKay replaced his log cabin with the ranch house. Soon after, he hired a Scottish girl, Jeannie Smith, to be his housekeeper. When the house was complete, the MacKays threw a housewarming party.

The MacKay residence became famous for its numerous lively parties. The ranch kitchen and dining room was a busy place as Jeannie cooked for the MacKays, their ranch hands, and for the many guests who visited.

The house was donated to Heritage Park in 1964 and was restored to the appearance of a typical farmhouse belonging to a family of British origin, as indicated by the polo mallets, antler furniture, and taxidermy mounts. Alex MacKay's son, James, established the famous MacKay's Ice Cream shop in Cochrane.

RECTORY

Built in 1899, near Carseland

A rectory — residence of the protestant minister — was a luxury few parishes could afford to supply their clergymen. Despite being modest in the extreme, it was a busy centre of community activity.

The minister's wife had many responsibilities including entertaining guests and supporting the women in the community. Her kitchen and parlour bustled with activity. In parishes with small churches, Sunday school classes, bible readings and prayer meetings might be held in the rectory. Church clubs such as the Ladies Aid Society would conduct meetings, and fundraising activities such as bake sales and teas may have taken place there. A parishioner could join the minister or his wife for an informational chat and cup of tea.

The Rectory

LIVINGSTON HOUSE

Built in 1883 on current Heritage Park land

Samuel Henry Harkwood Livingston was born in Ireland in 1831. In 1847, he left Ireland for New York, and in 1849 he went to California to take part in the gold rush. After the rush ended, Sam continued to prospect in rivers and creeks all over the western half of North America.

In 1865, while visiting the Victoria settlement near Edmonton he met Jane Howse, a 16-year old Métis girl. They married that same year. They set up a trading post at Jumping Pound Creek west of Calgary in 1873. By 1875, Sam and Jane were living near the confluence of the Bow and Elbow Rivers, but they moved upstream in about 1878 when the Northwest Mounted Police arrived. There, Sam built a sturdy cabin for his family.

71

During construction, Sam's family remained in their house near the police Fort due to the increasing threat of Indian rebellion.

In 1883, Sam built a 2-storey log house to accommodate his growing family, which would eventually number 14 children. The Livingstons' former residence was converted into a granary, but would also be used as a bunkhouse, a barn, and later as a garage.

Livingston House

Sam Livingston was a hardworking and innovative farmer who regularly had impressive yields from his grain crops, and who was known for growing huge vegetables in his garden. He imported Calgary's first binder, mower, hay rake, and threshing machine, and he even attempted to grow apples on his farm.

Sam's wife, Jane Howse, was the daughter of a prominent Hudson's Bay Company Factor, and a woman of many skills.

She welcomed new settler women to Calgary and helped them learn to survive in the early west.

Sam and Jane entertained many prominent visitors, and their home was a welcoming place for all who passed by.

Discover *How the West was Once*® with
a visit to Heritage Park Historical Village.

1900 Heritage Drive S.W.
Calgary, Alberta, Canada T2V 2X3
403-268-8500
www.heritagepark.ca

Made in the USA
Charleston, SC
08 July 2016